Exploring Science 4

Penny Johnson
Mark Levesley

Edinburgh Gate
Harlow, Essex

Contents

How to use this book

You should be able to answer this question by the time you have finished the work on the page.

This box has interesting facts about science.

Some questions are spread around the page, so you can answer them as you work through the page.

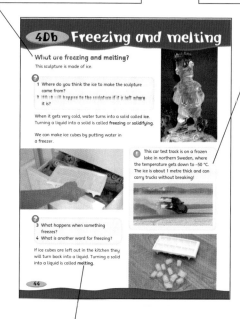

You can find out what words in **bold** mean by looking in the glossary at the end of the book.

These boxes give you ideas for practical work.

These boxes remind you of what you should have learned from the page.

The questions in this box will help you to plan your investigation.

This question helps you to think about what you will be investigating.

The children are talking about how they are going to do the investigation. Some of them have good ideas, but some of the ideas may not be very good!

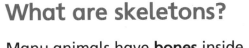

What are skeletons?

Many animals have **bones** inside them. Their bones form a **skeleton**. The pictures show the skeletons of four different animals.

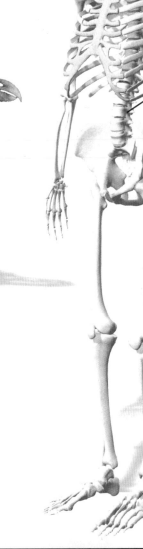

B

backbone (spine)

A

backbone

ribs

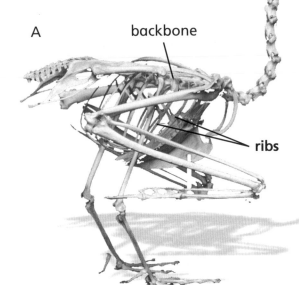

C

skull   backbone

D   backbone   fin bones

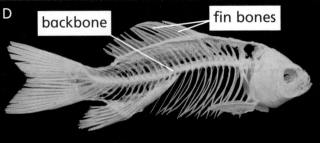

Some parts of the skeletons of different animals are similar and some parts are different. For instance, all the skeletons shown here have a **backbone** or **spine**, but only one has fin bones.

?

1 The animals that the skeletons on page 4 came from are:
   - a bird called a gull
   - a dinosaur called *Tyrannosaurus rex*
   - a fish
   - a human.

   Which picture letter matches each animal?

2 Do fish have ribs?

3 Write down two things that are the same in all the skeletons.

4 Describe two things that are different between skeletons B and D.

5 a Which do you think are stronger, fish bones or human bones?

   b Why do you think this?

! You have 270 bones but adults only have 206. As you get older some of your bones join together.

Most bones are hard and strong, but thicker bones are stronger than thinner ones.

Even thick bones may break if they are hit very hard. If you break a bone it can be very painful and you will need to go to hospital. In hospital, an X-ray photograph is taken, which allows doctors to see your bones.

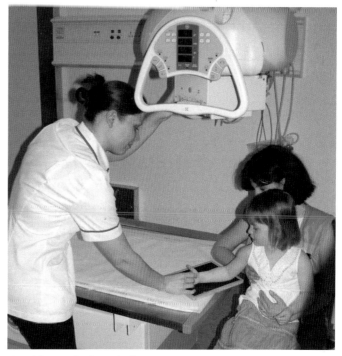

An X-ray being taken.

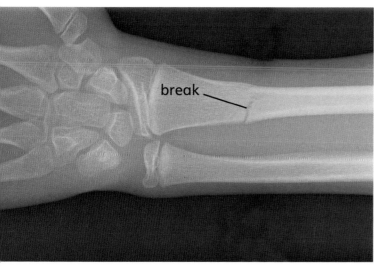

break

An X-ray photograph.

Now you should know...

- Some animals have skeletons made of bones.
- Where the spine, ribs and skull are in a human.

6 Write down the names of three bones found in humans.

7 What part of the body is shown in the X-ray photograph?

8 Find out how doctors mend broken bones.

What information can old bones give us?

Bones are very hard and they don't rot away quickly when they are buried underground. They are often dug up again many years later, and these bones can give scientists useful information.

Studying how people used to live

When skeletons are found, scientists measure the sizes of the bones. This can tell them whether a skeleton belonged to a man or a woman, how old and how tall the person was. Using this information, scientists have discovered that the average height of a British man one thousand years ago was 173 cm, 200 years ago it was 167 cm and today it is 177 cm.

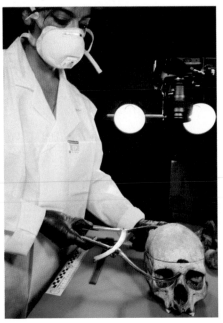
A scientist measuring the bones in a skeleton.

?

1 Some skeletons of people who died thousands of years ago can be found underground. Only their bones are found, not their skin or other parts. Why is this?

2 a Were men in 1066 generally taller or shorter than they were in 1766?

  b How can scientists tell how tall a person was from a skeleton?

Using skeletons, scientists can also tell things about the way people lived.

right arm   left arm

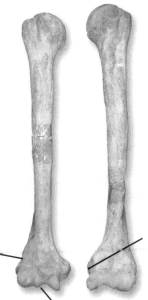

This bone is very thick at the bottom showing that it was used for pulling things.

This bone has a piece missing here – a common injury in archers.

elbow

The shapes of these upper arm bones tell scientists that this man was an archer.

Scientists can also find out things about how people died.

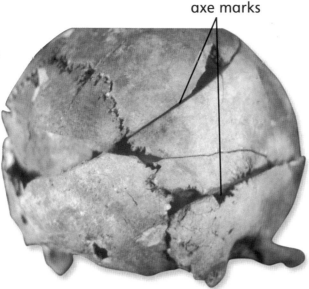

axe marks

This is the skull of a soldier killed at the battle of Towton on 29 March 1461. Scientists can tell that he was killed by being hit on the head twice with an axe.

?

3 Look at the photograph on the left. What do the slits in the skull tell us?

4 You need to eat a balanced diet to have strong, thick bones. What do you think the skeleton of someone who did not eat a balanced diet might look like?

Studying animals that no longer exist

The bones from animals can also be found. These are sometimes from animals that are **extinct** (don't exist any more) and can be *millions* of years old. For example, the oldest dinosaur bones ever found were 230 million years old.

The bones of extinct animals can help to tell us what they looked like.

These are the bones of a dinosaur called a sauropod that died over 100 million years ago.

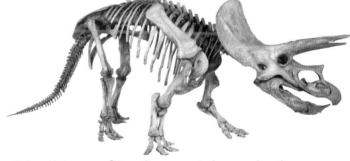

Scientists can fit a dinosaur's bones back together to form its skeleton. This is the skeleton of a triceratops.

?

5 What does the word 'extinct' mean?
6 About how many years ago did the sauropod live on Earth?
7 Look at the photograph of the model of the triceratops. Why can't scientists be sure what colour it was?

Using the skeleton, scientists can have a good guess at what a triceratops looked like.

What happens to your skeleton as you get older?

This X-ray photograph shows a family.

?

1 Look at the X-ray photograph. Which person has the longest leg bones?
2 What happens to the lengths of your leg bones as you get older?

The pictures show Mark at different ages. As he got older his skeleton grew and so he got taller. However, once Mark was 18 he stopped growing.

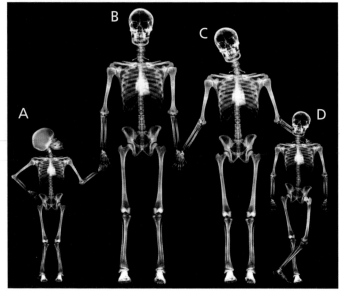

An X-ray photograph of a family.

?

3 a How does Mark's height change as he gets older?
  b Write the name of one bone that causes this change.
4 a How does the distance around Mark's head change as he gets older?
  b Which bone causes this change?
5

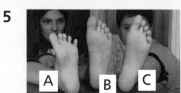

  a Which foot is the oldest?
  b Why do you think this?

Mark at age 2, age 13 and as an adult.

Now you should know...

• Your skeleton grows until you are an adult.

How can you compare the sizes of a body part?

People's skeletons are different sizes and so the parts of their bodies are different sizes. You are going to compare the sizes of one part of people's bodies. You need to plan an investigation to do this.

P

What questions about the sizes of body parts could you investigate?

- Come up with a list in your group.
- Then choose one question to investigate.

What you think you are going to find out in your investigation is called a **prediction**.

- Write down your prediction.

> I wonder how our body measurements compare with adults'.

> We could compare the sizes of people's feet.

> I think boys have longer arms than girls.

> I don't think that the head size changes much as you get older.

> We need to turn our ideas into questions!

P

The information that you use to answer a question is called **evidence**. How will you get evidence to answer your investigation question?

- What will you measure?
- How will you do your measuring?
- How many people will you ask?
- Draw a table to record your results.

> We could ask people how long their legs are.

> We could use a ruler to measure arm lengths.

> We could use a tape measure to go around people's heads.

> We'll need to do a lot of measuring!

> I think we should draw a table and then draw a **bar chart**.

9

How do skeletons support and protect animals?

When a hand is inside a glove puppet, the puppet can sit up. Without the hand, the puppet is floppy. The hand supports the puppet, like your skeleton supports your body.

Animals that have skeletons inside them are called **vertebrates**. You could not sit, stand or hold out your arms without a skeleton.

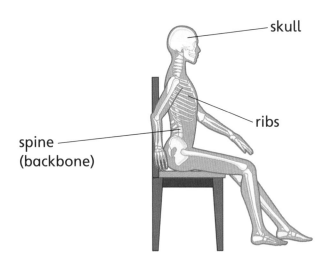

skull

ribs

spine (backbone)

> **?**
> 1 Write down the names of three vertebrates.
> 2 What are all the bones inside your body called?
> 3 Look at the picture. Which bone is supporting the girl so that she can sit up?

Animals without skeletons

The bodies of all animals need support, but some animals don't have skeletons like us. Animals like this are called **invertebrates**. A crab, for example, has a hard outer covering rather than hard bones inside it.

A crab.

An earthworm.

A worm has no hard parts. Its body is made of sections full of a watery liquid, which help the worm keep its shape.

4 a Describe three ways in which animals support their bodies.
  b Write the name of one animal which uses each type of support.
5 a How do you think a slug supports its body?
  b Why do you think this?
6 What is an invertebrate?

Skeletons for protection

A worm is not protected from damage because it has no hard parts. The hard covering of a crab means that it is well protected. In humans, only some parts of our bodies are protected by bones. For example, ribs protect your lungs and heart.

! The tails of hermit crabs are quite soft, and so these crabs find old shells to put their bodies into for protection.

A hermit crab.

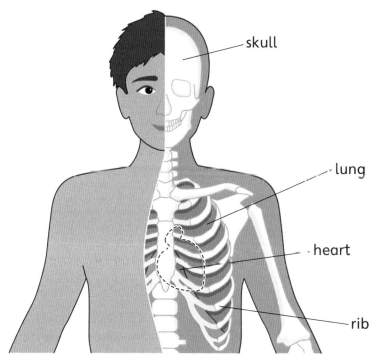

skull

lung

heart

rib

7 Which bones protect your heart and lungs?
8 Which bone protects your brain?
9 Why do you think snails need shells?

Now you should know...

- Some of your bones are for support.
- Some of your bones are for protection.
- Some animals don't have skeletons like us and have to support their bodies in other ways.

How do our skeletons allow us to move?

Although the bones in your arms are not bendy, you *can* bend your arms. Each arm contains more than one bone and can bend where the bones meet. The parts of your body where bones meet and move are called **joints**.

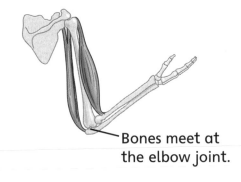

Bones meet at the elbow joint.

The bones in an arm.

> **?**
> 1 Write the name of the joint in the middle of your:
>   **a** arm   **b** leg.

Muscles

Muscles are parts of your body that can move other parts of your body. Your bones have muscles connected to them, and these muscles can move your bones.

> **?**
> 2 How can you tell that the man in the photograph has big arm muscles?
> 3 What do muscles do?

The drawing on the right shows two of the muscles in an arm – the **biceps** and **triceps**. When you lift your hand, the biceps muscle gets shorter and fatter as it pulls up the bones in the lower arm. When a muscle gets shorter and fatter, we say that it **contracts**.

To lift the hand, the biceps muscle contracts and the triceps muscle relaxes.

> **!** Your body contains many thousands of muscles but only 640 of them have names and not all of them are attached to bones. Your tongue, for instance, is made up of many muscles but no bones.

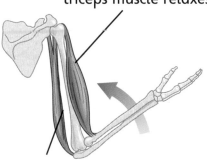

triceps muscle

When you lower your hand, the biceps gets longer and thinner again. We say that the muscle **relaxes**.

It takes effort for a muscle to contract but it does not take any effort for a muscle to relax.

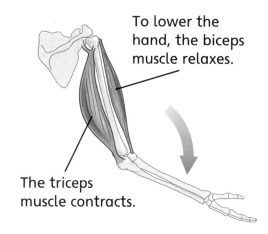

To lower the hand, the biceps muscle relaxes.

The triceps muscle contracts.

?

4 Write the names of two muscles in an arm.

5 What happens when a muscle contracts?

Muscles can only pull and cannot push. For this reason, muscles are found in pairs, with one muscle pulling a bone one way and another muscle pulling the bone in the other way.

The knee joint.

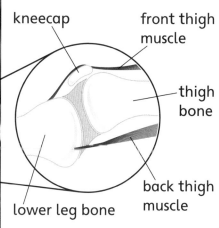

kneecap

front thigh muscle

thigh bone

back thigh muscle

lower leg bone

P

Earthworms also move using muscles but they don't have bones. How would you find out how earthworms move?

?

6 a Which leg muscle contracts to move the woman's lower leg up?

 b Which leg muscle contracts to move her leg down?

 c Why do muscles come in pairs?

What happens to muscles when you exercise?

When you do exercise your muscles work hard to move your body. As your muscles work, your body starts to feel different.

?

1 How do you think the runner feels at the end of her race? Think of three descriptive words.

P

How could you find out how much exercise you have to do before you start to feel different?
- What exercise could you do?
- What will you measure or observe?
- What do you think you will find? Make a prediction.

Exercise affects different people in different ways. Runners train hard to build stronger muscles so that they can do more exercise without getting too tired.

Exercise is good for you, and the more you exercise the fitter you become.

Paula Radcliffe winning the London Marathon. A marathon is 26 miles 285 yards long.

?

2 Why do runners need to train hard?
3 Why do you think someone might not finish the London Marathon?
4 a Who would be fitter, an office worker or a builder?
  b Why do you think this?

Now you should know…

- Your muscles work hard when you exercise and make you feel different.

What things can go wrong with muscles?

Muscles are attached to bones by strong cords called **tendons**. If a muscle is exercised too much, its tendon may swell up and become painful. This is called tendonitis (pronounced '*ten-don-I-tus*').

Strains and sprains

A strain occurs when a muscle or tendon is stretched too much and tears. This usually happens if someone suddenly does a lot of exercise when they are not used to it.

A sprain occurs when the cord connecting two bones together (a **ligament**) is stretched too much and tears. This is usually caused by an injury, such as a twisted ankle or twisted knee.

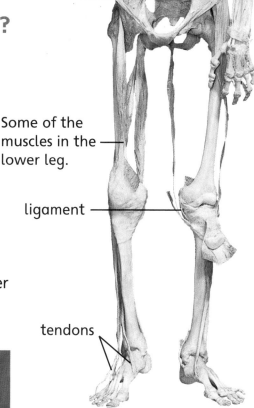

Some of the muscles in the lower leg.

ligament

tendons

Some parts of human legs.

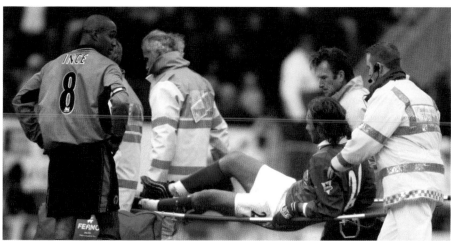

An injured footballer.

Muscular dystrophy

Muscular dystrophy (pronounced '**musk**-you-lar **diss**-trof-ee') is a disease that some people are born with. They have muscles that slowly get weaker and weaker.

This girl has muscular dystrophy.

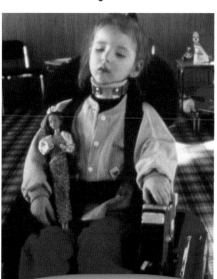

?

1 What does a tendon do?
2 a What is the difference between a sprain and a strain?
  b Is a footballer more likely to get a sprain or a strain? Explain your answer.
3 Why is the child with muscular dystrophy in a wheelchair?
4 Before exercising people should do stretches. Find out why.

What is an organism?

Anything that is living is called an **organism**. So, all plants and animals are organisms. There are millions of different kinds of organism.

Although different kinds of organisms do not look the same, they can all do some of the same things. For example, they can all **reproduce** (make new organisms) and **grow**.

?

1 What is an organism?

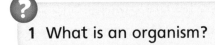
bluebells

cow

snail

woodlouse

duck

oak tree

?

2 Look at the pictures above. Write a list of all the:

  a animals   **b** plants.

3 Write down two things that all organisms can do.

Now you should know...

• An organism is a living thing.
• All organisms grow and reproduce.

What is a habitat?

Different organisms live in different places, called **habitats**. There are many different sorts of habitats but all habitats provide organisms with the things they need to live (such as food, water and shelter).

a flowerbed habitat

a woodland habitat

a habitat under a log

a pond habitat

a field habitat

?

1 Look at the organisms on page 16. Which habitat would each one live in?
2 Write down one habitat that is:
   a large   **b** small.
3 What do all habitats provide?
4 Why would a horse not live in a pond habitat?
5 What is your habitat?

Now you should know...

- The place where an organism lives is its habitat.
- A habitat provides shelter and food.

Studying habitats

What should you look for when you study a habitat?

Each kind of habitat is different. Some habitats are wet, while others are dry. Some habitats are full of light, while others are dark. Some habitats are hot and some are cold.

A desert habitat.

1 Describe what a desert habitat is like during the day.
2 Look at the habitats on page 17. Describe what each one is like on a summer day.

Scientists often collect small animals to study what lives in a certain habitat. Scientists use special ways of collecting animals to make sure that they don't hurt the animals. The animals are always returned to where they were found.

Some small animals can be collected using a soft paint brush and a container.

*You can use a net or jar to catch small animals in a pond. Doing this is called **pond dipping**.*

3 What is pond dipping?
4 Write down a list of rules for collecting animals from habitats.

Now you should know...

- How to describe habitats.
- How small animals can be collected without hurting them.

What are extreme habitats like?

Some organisms are found in habitats that are very difficult to live in.

Darkest

If you went to the deepest part of the Pacific Ocean there would be 11 kilometres of water above you – enough to squash you completely. No light from the Sun reaches this part of the Earth.

This octopus lives at the bottom of the ocean.

Driest

The Atacama desert in South America is the driest place on Earth. It only rains three or four times in every 100 years!

Tamarugo trees in the Atacama have very deep roots to find water far underground.

Coldest

In the Antarctic, it is dark from April until September, and temperatures can get as low as −75 °C. It is also very windy.

Antarctica.

?

1 Why would humans not survive at the bottom of the Pacific Ocean?

2 a What would scientists need to bring when visiting each habitat on this page?

  b In which months of the year would it be best to visit Antarctica?

3 How do tamarugo trees survive in the desert?

How is a key used?

Some organisms look very different to each other. Some look quite similar. We can put organisms into groups. The organisms that share the same features are put in the same group. For example, we can divide the organisms in the pictures into two groups – plants and animals.

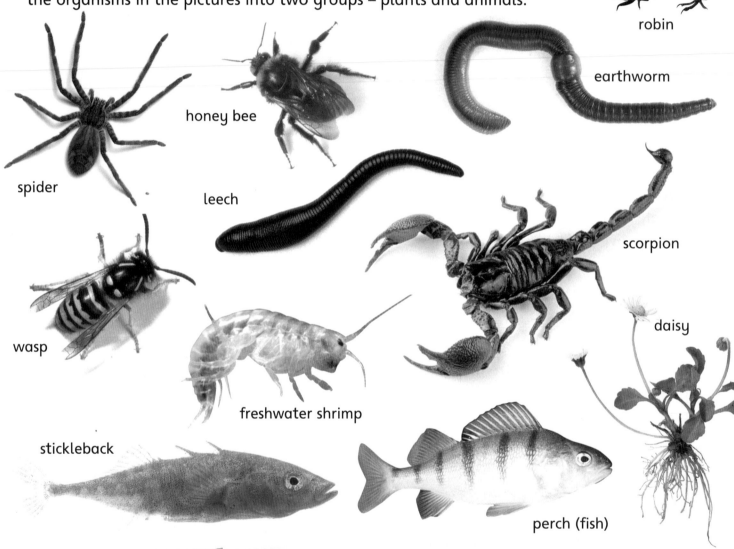

robin

earthworm

honey bee

spider

leech

scorpion

wasp

daisy

freshwater shrimp

stickleback

perch (fish)

dandelion

?

1 Look at the pictures. Write a list of the organisms that:
   a have eyes   b have wings   c have six legs.
2 Which organism is most similar to:
   a the wasp   b the daisy   c the spider?
3 Suggest a way of grouping the animals.

Often we need to find out the name of an organism. To do this we first need to look carefully at it.

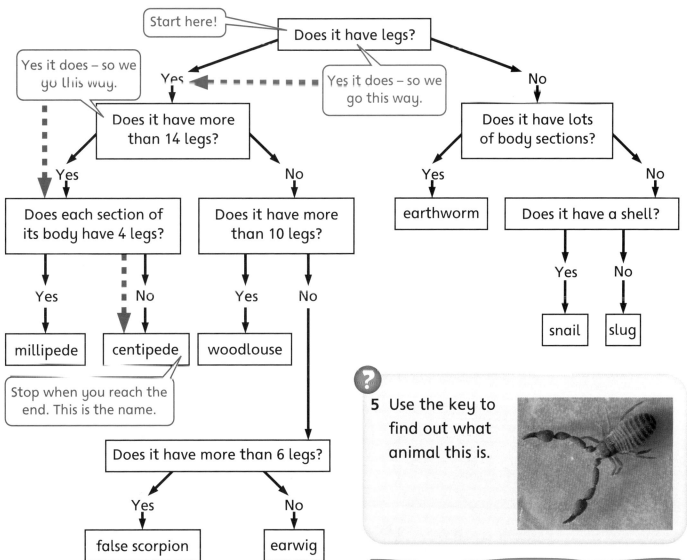

An animal found in a flowerbed habitat.

?
4 What does the animal in the photograph on the left look like? Describe two things.

We can use a **key** to help us to find out the name of this animal. Follow the blue lines on this key to see how it works.

Start here!

Does it have legs?

Yes it does – so we go this way.

Yes

Yes it does – so we go this way.

No

Does it have more than 14 legs?

Does it have lots of body sections?

Yes

No

Yes

No

Does each section of its body have 4 legs?

Does it have more than 10 legs?

earthworm

Does it have a shell?

Yes

No

Yes

No

Yes

No

millipede

centipede

woodlouse

snail

slug

Stop when you reach the end. This is the name.

Does it have more than 6 legs?

Yes

No

false scorpion

earwig

Key to small animals in flowerbeds.

?
5 Use the key to find out what animal this is.

Now you should know...

- Organisms with similar features can be grouped together.
- How to use a key.

How can we find out which places animals prefer?

Animals like to live in places where they can find food. Some animals find their food in damp places, some find food in dark places and others find food in warm places.

Earthworms find food in dark places.

P

What questions about animals and the places they prefer could you ask? Think about the factors you could change.
- Come up with a list of questions.
- Choose one question to investigate.
- Write down a prediction.

> My brother uses maggots for fishing. They seem to wriggle a lot when the lid of their pot is taken off.

> Where do earthworms live?

> Only some of the plants in my Gran's garden are eaten by snails.

> My Mum says that woodlice are good because they eat dead leaves and wood.

> We should leave the animals for a week and then see if they are still where we put them.

> We could put small animals in a container and watch where they go. They'll go to the areas they like straight away.

> We need a video camera to film the animals.

> We should leave the animals for a day and then count the numbers in each area.

P

How will you get evidence to answer your investigation question?
- What will you need?
- What will you do?
- How will you do a **fair test**? When you do a fair test you can only change one thing at a time.
- What will you observe or measure?
- How will you show your evidence?

How can we find out what animals eat?

All animals eat or 'consume' things and so they are called **consumers**. To find out what animals consume, scientists do experiments and carefully watch animals in their habitats.

Sometimes scientists find new kinds of animals, like this orange mouse. By watching it carefully the scientists discovered that it ate nuts.

This type of mouse was first discovered in a forest in the Philippines in 2004.

1 How did scientists find out what the orange mouse consumes?
2 The scientists who discover a new animal choose its name. What would you call this mouse?

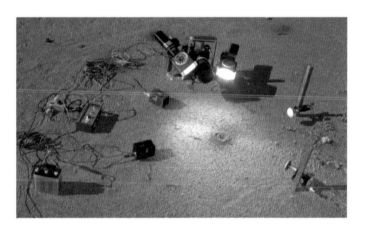

Photographs or videos provide good evidence about what a consumer eats. Some cameras can automatically take photographs, or start filming, only when an animal appears.

These cameras take photos automatically of a bee that burrows underground.

?

3 Look at the photograph of the thrush.
   a What do thrushes eat?
   b How do you know this?
4 Why are automatic cameras useful to scientists studying animals?

A thrush.

Now you should know...

• How scientists can find out what consumers eat.

What do food chains show?

All of these animals live in a woodland habitat. The different animals eat different things. Some eat plants and some eat other animals.

hedgehog   worm   fox   rabbit

Animals that eat other animals are called **predators**. All predators hunt other animals for food.

The animals that a predator hunts are called its **prey**. For example, foxes eat rabbits – the rabbits are prey for the foxes.

?

1 **a** Which two animals in the photographs above eat plants?
  b How do you know this?
2 Which of the animals in the photographs are predators?

! Some predators have some strange ways of hunting! This sawfish uses its long nose to slice through shoals of fish. The sawfish then eats the fish that it has wounded.

This great grey owl is about to catch and eat the vole.

We can show predators and their prey in a diagram. We use an arrow that points from the prey to the predator. The arrow means 'is eaten by'.

?

3 Look at the photograph of the owl on page 24.
   a Which animal is the predator?
   b Which animal is the prey?
4 Which animals are prey for:
   a foxes   **b** hedgehogs?

a vole   is eaten by   a great grey owl

Many animals that are prey are plant-eaters. For example, voles and rabbits both eat grass. We can add a plant to our diagram and make a **food chain**. A food chain shows what eats what and always starts with a plant.

grass   is eaten by   a vole   is eaten by   a great grey owl

?

5 Draw two food chains using the organisms at the top of page 24.

Now you should know...

• What predators and prey are.
• How to draw a food chain.

Changing habitats

What happens when humans change habitats?

Humans change many habitats by polluting them, destroying them or taking things from them.

Polluting habitats

In November 2002 a huge oil tanker sprang a leak in a storm about 150 miles off the coast of Spain. It soon broke in two and sank. It spilled about 64 000 tonnes of oil into the sea – enough to fill about 700 classrooms.

The oil tanker Prestige *sank off the coast of Spain on 19 November 2002.*

The oil poisoned millions of fish and small sea creatures. It also coated the feathers of sea birds, which meant that they could not fly and so they drowned. About 300 000 birds died.

A seabird coated in oil from the Prestige.

?

1 a What habitat was damaged when the oil tanker sank?

b What effect did the oil have on the animals in the habitat?

Destroying habitats

The photograph shows all that is left of a thick forest in Brazil. Humans have cut down the trees to get wood and to make fields. Many animals, like the red-handed tamarin, can't live there any more because there is no shelter or food.

?

2 Why are forests cut down?

3 Why can tamarins no longer live in areas where the forests have been cut down?

Red-handed tamarins eat buds, leaves and fruit.

Taking things from habitats

People have been catching fish in the North Sea for many years. Too many fish have been taken and now there are very few of some types of fish. Other animals can starve if there aren't enough fish to eat.

?

4 Here is a food chain from Mr Jones' pond.
   pond weed → great pond snail → great diving beetle
   What would happen if Mr Jones removed all the weed from his pond?

5 Here is a food chain from a sea habitat.
   tiny plants → tiny animals → sand eel → cod → seal
   What would happen if humans took too many cod from this habitat?

6 A park contains very old trees. The local newspaper has reported that some people want to cut the trees down. Write a letter to the newspaper saying what you think should happen and why.

Cut down dangerous trees says council

Now you should know...

- How humans change habitats.
- How changing a habitat affects the organisms living there.

What is temperature?

This mother is testing her baby's milk to feel how hot it is. Babies can only be given warm milk because hot milk can hurt them.

The mother is trying to measure the **temperature** of the milk by touching it. Temperature is how hot or cold something is. Hot things have higher temperatures than cold things.

1 Which will have the higher temperature, the baby's milk or milk from the fridge?

Some things can show us how hot or cold something is. The end of this baby spoon changes colour to yellow if the food is too hot for the baby. When the food is cool enough, the end of the spoon turns to red.

2 Look at the photograph of the baby food.
   a Is the food cool enough?
   b How can you tell this?
   c How could you test the food if you didn't have one of these spoons?

Now you should know...
- Hotter things have higher temperatures.

How can we measure temperatures?

Looking at something is not a good way of measuring its length. You need a ruler. As you go along a ruler, each line shows an increase in length of 1 centimetre.

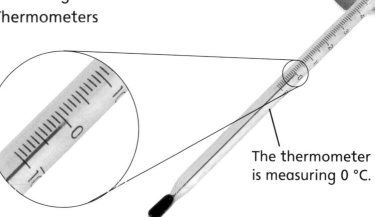

1 What does a ruler measure?

Feeling something is not a good way of measuring temperature. You need a **thermometer**. Thermometers measure temperatures in **degrees Celsius** (often written as **°C**). As you go up a thermometer, each little line shows a rise in temperature of 1 °C.

The thermometer is measuring 0 °C.

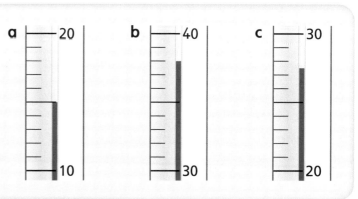

2 What does a thermometer measure?

3 What are the units for temperature?

4 Write out the following in words.

   a 10 °C

   b 21 °C

5 What temperatures are shown on these thermometers?

a 20 ... 10

b 40 ... 30

c 30 ... 20

Now you should know...

- You can measure temperatures using a thermometer.
- The units for temperature are degrees Celsius (°C).

How do temperatures change?

These potatoes will get hotter in the oven.

The potatoes will reach the same temperature as the air in the oven. When they are taken out, they will cool down to the same temperature as the air in the kitchen. All things heat up or cool down until they are the same temperature as their surroundings.

1 a What temperature will the potatoes be after 45 minutes?

b Why do you think this?

These potatoes are going into an oven at 200 °C.

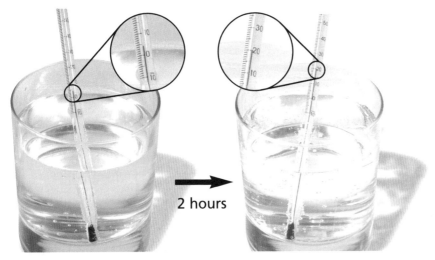

2 hours

This glass of cold lemonade was taken out of the fridge and left out for 2 hours.

One bowl in a classroom contains warm water and another contains icy water.

• How could you find out how their temperatures change in one hour?

• What do you think will happen? Make a prediction.

2 Look at the lemonade glass. What was the temperature of:

a the fridge

b the room?

Now you should know...

• Things heat up or cool down until they have the same temperature as their surroundings.

How do thermometers work?

When you heat things up, they get slightly bigger. They are said to **expand**.

ice water

warm water

The air in the balloon expands when it is heated

The air in this ball expands as it warms up.

One of the first thermometers was built in about 1593 by an Italian scientist called Galileo Galilei (1564–1642). As the air in the top ball expands it pushes down on the liquid in the tube.

liquid in tube

Galileo's first thermometer was called a thermoscope.

Modern thermometers use a liquid inside the rounded end of the thermometer (called the **bulb**). When the liquid is heated it expands and rises up the tube.

scale

Not all thermometers need something to expand. Some thermometers change colour instead.

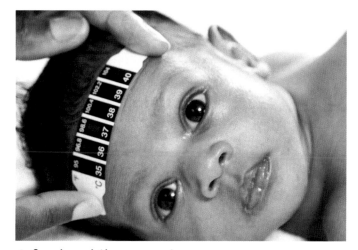

A forehead thermometer.

bulb

?

1 What does the word 'expand' mean?
2 Why does the balloon in the photographs get bigger?
3 a In Galileo's thermoscope, what happens to the level of the liquid when the temperature goes up?
   b Why does this happen?

How do we measure temperature changes?

This is a weather forecast map for a summer day. The circles tell you the temperature.

?

1 Look at the weather forecast map for a summer day.
   a What would the weather be like outside your school on this day?
   b What temperature would it be?

Weather forecast for a summer day.

At night it is colder because there is no sunlight.

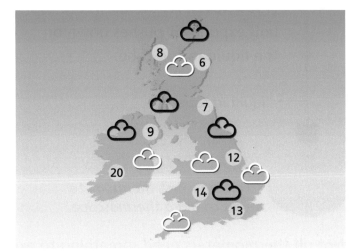

Weather forecast for a summer night.

It is also colder in winter and if it gets to 0 °C, or below, water can freeze. Temperatures below 0 °C have a minus sign in front of them. For example, −5 °C is 'minus five degrees Celsius' or 'five degrees below freezing'.

?

2 How is the temperature different:
   a at night compared with the day
   b in winter compared with summer?
3 At what temperature does water freeze?

Weather forecast for a winter day.

Many buildings use heating in the winter to keep the temperature inside at about 20 °C. This is called **room temperature** and is a temperature that most people find comfortable – neither too cold nor too hot.

Temperature changes are measured using thermometers or **temperature sensors** attached to computers. Temperature sensors can measure the temperature every hour and the computer records the results.

?

4 Some buildings have air conditioning to cool down the air. When would air conditioning be switched on?

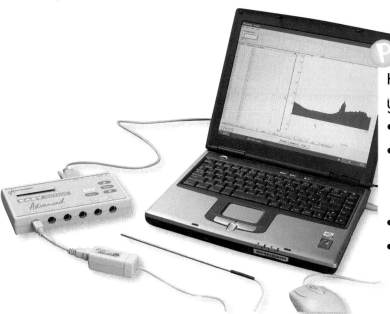

How does the temperature change in your classroom?

- Draw a map of your classroom.
- Mark two places where you will measure the temperature at different times of day.
- How will you measure the temperature?
- How do you think the temperature will change? Make a prediction.

Body temperature

Your **body temperature** is normally 37 °C. However, it can go up if you are ill and this is a good way of telling if someone is ill.

?

5 Why does a doctor take your temperature if you feel ill?
6 What do you think the temperature of your classroom is now?

Now you should know...

- Some common temperatures (for example, room temperature and body temperature).
- How temperature changes can be measured.

How can we keep things cold?

People who lived over 100 years ago did not have fridges, but rich families had ice houses. These were rooms dug into the ground. In winter, the servants cut ice from rivers, put it in an ice house and covered it in straw. The straw and the earth around the ice house helped stop the ice melting.

? **1** Why did ice take a long time to melt in an ice house?

An ice house.

! Alexander the Great was an army commander who lived about 2300 years ago. He made his slaves fetch ice from high mountains so that he could have cold drinks!

The ice houses were used to supply ice for drinks and to make ice cream. They were also used as places to store meat and fish to stop them going off.

? **2** Where do we store meat and fish in our homes today?

If a winter was not cold enough, there would be a shortage of ice. Between about 1820 and 1920 ice used to be brought on ships from the USA and Norway. This ice was stored in deep wells in warehouses and each day some of this ice was delivered to people's houses.

3 Why was ice expensive?
4 Why was Norway a good place to import ice from?

Ice being cut from a lake in the USA.

An ice delivery cart in about 1916.

Ice delivery people had to make sure their ice didn't melt!

- How could you stop an ice cube melting?
- How could you see if your idea worked?

Now you should know...

- Some materials can keep things cool.

Which material is best at keeping water warm?

A hot drink helps to keep you warm on a cold day. We need to use materials for cups and flasks that can keep drinks warm.

P

How can you find out which material is best at keeping water warm?

- Which materials will you test?
- How will you test the materials?
- What will you measure?
- How will you make your investigation fair? To do a **fair test** you should only change one thing and keep everything else the same.
- What do you think the best material is going to be? Make a **prediction**.

We should measure the temperatures of water in the cups after a day.

We must make sure that the water in the cups is the same temperature.

Thicker materials will work better than thinner ones.

My dad wraps some of the plants in the garden in black plastic for the winter.

I think the colour makes a difference since my winter clothes are dark colours.

Are different materials needed to keep things at different temperatures?

Some people put coverings around bottles of drink to keep them cool for longer. Some people put coverings around their cups of coffee or tea to keep them hot for longer.

This covering keeps the drink hot for longer.

This covering keeps the drink cold for longer.

Both coverings in the photographs are the same material (called neoprene). Materials that stop cold things getting hot too quickly also stop hot things getting cold too quickly.

?

1 Here are some materials.

   foam rubber   paper   plastic sheet   tea towel

   Foam rubber is the best for keeping cold things cold.

   a Which material would be best for keeping hot things hot?

   b Why do you think this?

2 This flask can be used to keep hot drinks hot.

   a Could it also be used for cold drinks?

   b Explain why you think this.

Now you should know...

- Materials that keep hot things hot can also be used to keep cold things cold.

What are thermal insulators and conductors?

When something gets hotter, heat flows *into* it. This pizza is getting hotter because heat from the oven is going into it.

?

1 Why does the pizza in the oven get hotter?

When something gets colder, heat flows *out* of it. The cooked pizza is now out of the oven. It is getting colder because heat is flowing out of it into the air. It keeps getting cooler until it reaches the temperature of the room.

?

2 Why does the cooked pizza get colder when it is taken out of the oven?

Heat always flows from a hotter thing to a colder thing. Materials that stop heat flowing from one thing to another are **thermal insulators**. (The word 'thermal' means 'heat'.)

?

3 What is a thermal insulator?

P

These three spoons have been put into hot water.

• How could you find out which spoons are good thermal insulators?

Thermal insulators don't allow heat to flow through them easily. Plastic, wood and things that trap air in them are all good thermal insulators. Bubble-wrap, neoprene and foam rubber all contain trapped air.

Thermal conductors

Things that let heat go through them easily are said to be **thermal conductors**. Metals are good thermal conductors.

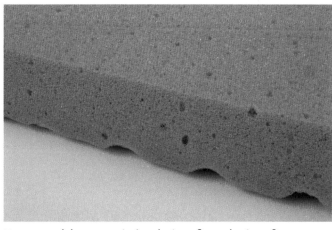

Foam rubber contains lots of pockets of trapped air.

The saucepan is made of metal so that heat can go easily from the cooker into the food in the pan.

4 a Why are saucepans made of metal?
  b Why are saucepan handles made of plastic.
5 Why do the carrots in the saucepan get hotter?
6 Why are oven gloves made out of a thermal insulator?

Electrical conductors

Things that let heat through them easily will also let electricity through them easily. That's why electrical wires are made of metal. Metals are good **electrical conductors**.

7 Why are electrical wires not made from plastic?

Now you should know...

- Heat always flows from a hotter thing to a colder thing.
- Thermal conductors let heat flow through them easily.
- Thermal insulators don't let heat through them easily.

How are solids and liquids different and similar?

A **property** describes something about a material. For example, brick is hard.

?

1 Write down two properties of brick.

These photographs show many different materials. They all have different properties that we can use to put the materials into groups. For example, honey and gold could be in a group of things that are yellow.

coal

diamond

gold

honey

metal

motor oil

plastic

shampoo

wood

water

?

2 Choose one material from the photographs. Describe its properties.
3 Think of a way of putting all the items in the photograph into just two groups.
  a Write down the names of your two groups.
  b Which materials go into each group?

There are many different properties that a material can have. The table on the right shows some of them.

Some materials can be poured and do not have fixed shapes. For example, water changes shape when it is poured from one container to another. Materials like this are **liquids**.

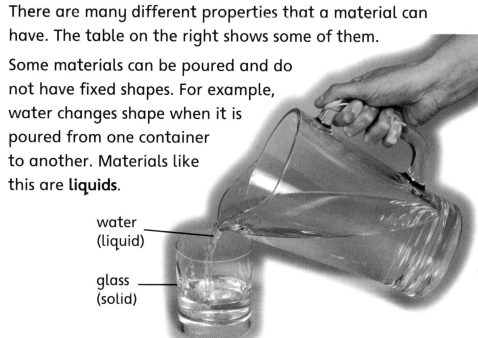

water (liquid)

glass (solid)

| brittle |
| changes shape |
| colour |
| electrical conductor |
| flexible (bendy) |
| hard |
| runny |
| strong |
| thermal conductor |
| transparent (see-through) |

Some common properties.

Some materials do not flow and have shapes that are fixed. For example, a glass does not change its shape on its own. Materials like this are **solids**.

?

4 Write down one property of:
   a solids
   b liquids.

5 Write down whether the things in these photographs are solids or liquids.

cooking oil

cotton wool

rice

sand

sponge

suntan lotion

Now you should know...

- Properties describe what a material is like.
- Solids have fixed shapes.
- Liquids do not have fixed shapes.

Measuring volumes

How can we measure the volume of a liquid?

Solids and liquids both take up space. The amount of space something takes up is its **volume**. We can measure the volume of a liquid by pouring it into a **measuring cylinder** or measuring jug.

To find the volume you need to look where the liquid level is on the scale. Volumes are measured in **millilitres,** or **ml** for short.

measuring cylinder

Keep your eye level with the top of the liquid. Find the part of the scale that is in line with the flat part of the liquid's surface. This volume is 300 ml.

Ignore any water that curves up at the edges.

300

250

200

How to use a measuring cylinder.

?

1 What is a volume?

P

Do liquids change volume when they change shape?
- How would you find out?
- What do you think you will find? Make a prediction.

?

2 What does ml stand for?

3 What is the volume of water in these measuring cylinders?

a

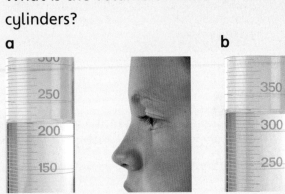

300
250
200
150

b

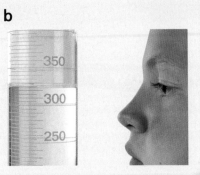

350
300
250

Now you should know...

- How to measure the volume of a liquid.

How are some solids like liquids?

Liquids can be poured but so can some solids.

water

water wheel

sand

?

1 a Suggest one way that sand is like water.

b Suggest one way that sand is not like water.

P

What do you think will happen if sand and water are poured through this material? Make a prediction.

Sand can flow because it is made of very tiny pieces. However, if you look at each tiny piece you will see that it is a solid. Although a load of sand can change shape, each tiny piece of sand keeps its shape.

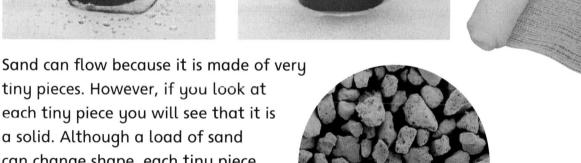

These are some of the pieces that make up sand. They are shown 30 times bigger here than in real life.

?

2 Why is sand said to be a solid?

3 What other solid materials can you think of that can act like liquids?

Now you should know...

• Some solids can flow because they are made of tiny pieces.

What are freezing and melting?

This sculpture is made of ice.

> **?**
>
> 1 Where do you think the ice to make the sculpture came from?
> 2 What will happen to the sculpture if it is left where it is?

When it gets very cold, water turns into a solid called **ice**. Turning a liquid into a solid is called **freezing** or **solidifying**.

We can make ice cubes by putting water in a freezer.

> **!** This car test track is on a frozen lake in northern Sweden, where the temperature gets down to −50 °C. The ice is about 1 metre thick and can carry trucks without breaking!
>
>

> **?**
>
> 3 What happens when something freezes?
> 4 What is another word for freezing?

If ice cubes are left out in the kitchen they will turn back into a liquid. Turning a solid into a liquid is called **melting**.

Ice melts easily but other solids need to be heated to get them to melt.

Chocolate will melt in your hands.

Gold needs to be heated to a very high temperature (over 1000 °C) to get it to melt.

Candle wax melts in the heat from a flame.

Reversible changes

Something that has melted can be frozen again and something that has frozen can be melted again. Freezing and melting are changes that can be reversed. They are **reversible changes**.

Now you should know...

- Changing from a liquid to a solid is called freezing or solidifying.
- Changing from a solid to a liquid is called melting.
- Freezing and melting are reversible changes.

5 **a** Write a list of four materials mentioned on these pages.
   b Put the materials in order of the temperatures at which they melt. Start with the one that melts the easiest.

6 Describe the properties of gold when it is:
   a solid   **b** liquid.

7 Why do you think it is useful to melt gold?

8 Freezing is a reversible change. What does this mean?

How easily do different cooking materials melt?

Many things are cooked in melted butter, margarine or fat.

P

How would you find out how easily each of these materials melts?

- How will you test the materials?
- What will you measure?
- How will you make your investigation fair?
- Which material do you think will be easiest to melt? Make a prediction.
- Why do you think this material is easiest to melt?

We must make sure we use the same amount of each material.

The more yellow the material it is, the easier it will melt.

Will those cake cups float on water?

My Mum only uses solid vegetable fat in her cooking. Maybe that's because it melts so quickly in the pan.

I always watch my Dad cooking and I have never noticed a difference between how quickly these things melt.

What are melting and freezing points?

Frozen water.

Water freezes at 0 °C and below. We say that 0 °C is the **freezing point** of water.

Ice melts at 0 °C and above. The **melting point** of water is 0 °C. The freezing point and melting point of a material are the same temperature.

?

1 What is a freezing point?
2 The freezing point of gold is 1064 °C. What is its melting point?
3 Imagine the materials in the table are all at 0 °C. Write down the order in which they melt if you warm them up.

Material	Freezing point (°C)
butter	32
candle wax	65
chocolate	36
copper	1083
sugar	146

At exactly 0 °C there are equal amounts of water and ice – the ice is melting and the water is freezing! Below 0 °C all the water will freeze and above 0 °C all the ice will melt.

Now you should know...

• The freezing point and melting point of a material are the same temperature.

How can you separate mixtures of solids?

When you jumble up different materials you end up with a **mixture**.

Some different mixtures made of solids.

?

1 Why is the bag of vegetables a mixture?

To un-jumble a mixture you need to **separate** the different things in it. You can separate out the different vegetables in mixed vegetables using your fingers. You can separate sand from marbles using a **sieve**. When you use a sieve it is called **sieving**.

When sieving, you need to choose a sieve with holes big enough to let one thing through but not another.

Using a sieve to separate marbles from sand.

P

How could you separate this mixture? Write a list of instructions.

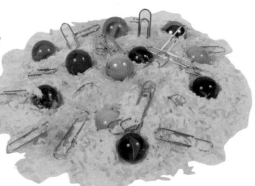

?

2 What is sieving?

Now you should know...

• How sieving can separate solids from a mixture.

What happens when you mix solids with water?

Lots of mixtures contain water but different solids do different things when water is added. For instance, gravy granules turn the water brown and disappear.

? **1 a** What are the different materials that are mixed to make the gravy?

b Which material was solid?

c Which material was liquid?

d What happens to the liquid?

If water is added to buttons, the water stays the same colour and you can still see the buttons.

P

What do you think will happen when water is added to these materials?

instant coffee   powder paint

sugar   plaster of Paris   sand

• How would you find out if you are right?

? **2** Describe two different things that can happen when a solid is mixed with water.

Now you should know...

• Different things happen when different solids are mixed with water.

How can solids be separated from liquids?

We can separate some solids from liquids using a sieve. You can use this sieve to separate marbles from water.

If you use the same sieve to separate sand and water, it doesn't work.

1 a Why can't you separate sand and water using this sieve?
b What could you use to separate sand and water?

The sieve holes are too big to separate sand from water and the sand goes through the holes. We need something with smaller holes. Kitchen towels have tiny holes that you can't see.

Using something with holes to separate a solid from a liquid is called **filtering** and the thing you use (for example, the kitchen towel) is called a **filter**.

2 What is filtering?
3 Why does kitchen towel let water through but not sand?

Using kitchen towel to filter a mixture of sand and water.

Now you should know...

- You can separate some solids from liquids by filtering.

What are the properties of mixtures like?

Winston Churchill was Prime Minister during the Second World War. One day, in 1942, one of his advisers, Lord Mountbatten, burst into Churchill's bathroom and dropped a piece of ice into the Prime Minister's bath! Churchill didn't get angry. He just stared at the ice because it wasn't melting. It was a new invention, called Pykrete, which was a mixture of ice and sawdust. Pykrete took a long time to melt and was very strong.

Churchill was impressed and ordered ships to be made from Pykrete. Testing was done in Canada but by the time this was finished the war was being won, and so Pykrete ships were never built.

Winston Churchill

Lord Mountbatten

A Pykrete boat being tested in 1943.

?

1 How were the properties of Pykrete different to the properties of:
   a ice
   b sawdust?
2 Are the properties of mixtures the same as the materials in them?
3 Find out who invented Pykrete.

4Dd Dissolving

What happens when a solid dissolves?

The bottle contains sea water. You can see it is a mixture because you can see water and sand. However, there is something else in sea water that you can't see.

Sea water.

> **?**
>
> 1 a How can you see that sea water is a mixture?
>   b What material does sea water contain that you can't see?

When you add some materials to water, they seem to disappear. Sea water contains salt which you cannot see, but the salt is still there.

George, that was salt you put in my tea!

> **?**
>
> 2 How could you tell if there is salt in some water?

If a substance seems to disappear when you put it into water we say that it **dissolves**. Salt dissolves in water. When a solid dissolves in a liquid, the liquid becomes a mixture called a **solution**. Sea water is a solution of salt and water.

> **?**
>
> 3 Write down the name of another material that dissolves in water.
> 4 What is a solution?

Do you think that salt can be separated from sea water using a filter?
- What would you do to find out?
- How would you test the liquid that comes through the filter?
- What do you think will happen? Make a prediction.

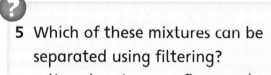

Some materials remain **undissolved** in water but dissolve in other liquids. For example, nail polish will not dissolve in water but will dissolve in acetone (nail polish remover).

When a solid dissolves, it splits up into very tiny particles. These particles spread out in the water so that you can no longer see them. The particles are so small that they easily fit through filters with even the smallest of holes. You cannot separate a dissolved solid from a solution.

All solutions are transparent but sometimes they have a colour because the tiny dissolved particles have a colour. Tiny tea particles give black tea a colour but black tea is still a solution.

Salty water has no colour but black tea is a coloured solution.

5 Which of these mixtures can be separated using filtering?

salt and water   flour and water

sand and water   sugar and water

6 Which of these mixtures are solutions?

sugary   milk   aspirin   lime   sandy
water   in water   cordial   water

7 How can you tell if something dissolves in water?

Now you should know...

- Some solids dissolve in water to form transparent solutions.
- You cannot get a dissolved solid out of a solution by filtering.

How do we measure forces?

Forces can be pushes...   or pulls.

We can show the direction of forces using arrows.

If you pull on a spring, it stretches. If you pull it with a bigger force, it gets even longer.

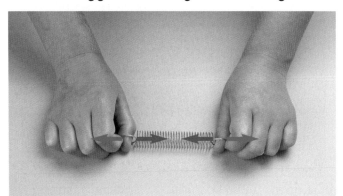

A small force.

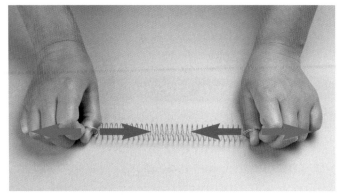

A bigger force.

?

1

Ben

Abdul

a Why are the springs in the picture stretching?

b Who is putting the biggest force on the springs?

c Explain how you decided on your answer to part **b**.

We can use springs to measure forces. A **forcemeter** has a spring inside it. You can read the size of the force from the scale.

Forces are measured in units called **newtons**. We can write newtons as **N**, for short.

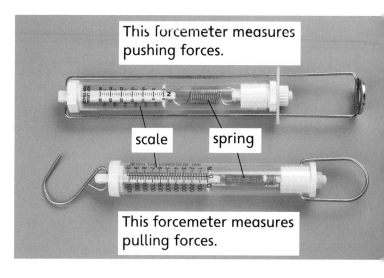

This forcemeter measures pushing forces.

scale   spring

This forcemeter measures pulling forces.

?

2 a What does a forcemeter do?

  b What does it have inside it?

3 What are the units for forces?

If you pull with a small force, the spring in the forcemeter only stretches a little way.

If you pull with a bigger force, the spring stretches further.

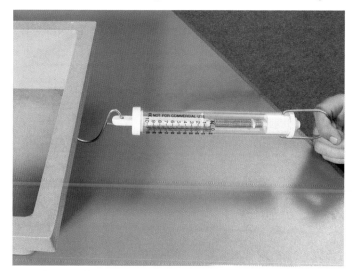

It takes a force of 1 N to drag this tray along the table.

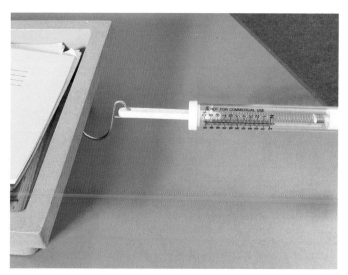

The tray is heavier. It takes a force of 9 N to drag it along the table.

?

4 Look at the picture in question 1. Abdul is pulling with a force of 20 N.

  a How much force is Ben using? Choose the correct answer.

    A more than 20 N

    B exactly 20 N

    C less than 20 N

  b Explain how you worked out your answer.

Now you should know...

- Forces are measured using a forcemeter.
- The units for measuring forces are newtons (N).

Investigating friction

Which surfaces have high friction?

Sometimes it is very difficult to push things.
The force that stops things sliding is called **friction**.

There is a lot of friction between the box and the floor.

P

Which surfaces allow objects to slide most easily?

- How can you test different surfaces?
- How can you make your test fair?
- How will you present your results?

> We could test different shoes instead of different surfaces.

> We could see how steep we have to make the ramp before it starts to slide.

> There will be less friction on a smooth floor than on a rough one.

> We should pull the same thing each time to make sure our test is fair.

> We should measure the force it takes to get the box moving.

When is friction useful?

Friction is a force that stops things sliding, or makes it difficult for things to slide. Sometimes it is important to have high friction.

You need friction between your shoes and the ground to stop you slipping.

Cars and bicycles need a lot of friction between their tyres and the road to stop them skidding.

Sometimes we do not want much friction.

Slides are made from materials with low friction.

1 When do we need a lot of friction?
2 Goalkeepers wear gloves. Why do they need a lot of friction between their gloves and the ball?

3 What would happen if a slide had high friction?

How could you find the best material for clothes to wear on a slide?

Now you should know...

• When we need a lot of friction.
• When friction is not useful.

Which surfaces have the highest friction?

We need friction between our shoes and the floor to help us to walk. It can be difficult to walk on very smooth floors, because they are slippery. Smooth surfaces have low friction.

The tyres on cars and bicycles need to grip the road so they do not slip. The material used to make roads has a rough surface. Rough surfaces have high friction.

We can make surfaces even smoother by polishing them.

There was not enough friction between this car and the road!

The slide is made from polished, shiny metal. The seats on the swing are made from plastic, which is not very smooth.

?

1 Which has the highest friction, a rough surface or a smooth surface?
2 How can we make a smooth surface even smoother?
3 Why should roads have rough surfaces?
4 Why is the slide made from smooth metal?
5 Why aren't the swing seats made from a smooth material?

Now you should know...

- Rough surfaces have higher friction than smooth ones.

What is lubrication?

Wet floors can be very slippery, because the water reduces the friction between your feet and the floor. The water is a **lubricant**.

Lubrication is important whenever we want surfaces to move over each other easily. Lubricants like **oil** help the parts inside engines to move easily.

We put oil into car engines.

Oil helps bicycle wheels to turn easily.

Sometimes lubrication is a problem. Car tyres need to grip the road, but if it has been raining there may be water on the road. The water lubricates the tyres, so they are more likely to slip.

Dangerous driving conditions!

?

1 a What is a lubricant?
  b Why do we put oil into engines?
  c Why do bicycles need oiling?
2 It can be difficult to hold glasses or plates when your hands are wet. Why is this?
3 Why is driving more dangerous when the road is wet?

What is water resistance?

It is difficult to walk in water, because the water seems to push against you when you move. This force is called **water resistance**.

?

1 Why is it difficult to walk through water?

Lucy can walk much faster than Omar because there is no water resistance pushing against her.

Water resistance is a kind of friction. It is a force that tries to slow down anything that moves through water. We can change the amount of water resistance by changing the shape of an object.

Dolphins have smooth shapes to help them to swim fast.

These boats have pointed fronts and smooth shapes to make their water resistance less.

?

2 Why do boats have pointed front ends?
3 Why do fish have smooth shapes?
4 Which shape has the lowest water resistance?

A 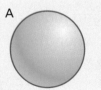   B    C

Now you should know...

• Water resistance is a force that slows down objects moving through water.
• Smooth shapes have less water resistance.

4Ec Investigating water resistance

Which shapes have the lowest water resistance?

P

Which shapes have the lowest water resistance?
- How can you find out?
- What apparatus will you need?
- How will you make sure your test is fair?

Air resistance

What is air resistance?

Air is all around us, but we cannot see it. We can feel the air on a windy day.

The larger the object, the harder the air pushes on it. Big things have a higher **air resistance** than small things, so the wind pushes on them harder.

The force of the wind has blown this tree over and damaged the car.

Julie's umbrella is small, so there is not much force on it. Ben has a much bigger umbrella. There is a very big force on it from the wind.

Air resistance is a kind of friction. It slows down things moving through air.

?

1 a Why is it difficult to use a big umbrella on a windy day?

b Why is it easier to use a small umbrella?

Parachutes need a lot of air resistance.

This Tornado aeroplane flies very fast. It needs to have a low air resistance.

2 What does air resistance do to things moving through air?

3 Why do parachutes need a large air resistance?

4 **a** Why does the Tornado aeroplane need a low air resistance?

   b How do you think the shape of the aeroplane gives it a low air resistance?

5 Look at the aeroplane on the right.

   a Do you think this aeroplane flies fast or slowly?

   b Why do you think this?

! Some small aeroplanes have parachutes in them, in case something goes wrong. The parachute will make sure the areoplane lands safely by bringing it down slowly.

P Does the size of a parachute affect how long it takes to fall?

• How can you find out?

• How will you make your test fair?

Now you should know...

• Air resistance is a kind of friction.

• It slows down things moving through air.

• There is more air resistance on large objects.

Why are some things streamlined?

A **streamlined** shape is a smooth shape that air or water can flow past easily. The more streamlined a shape is, the lower the air resistance or water resistance.

You can feel air resistance when you ride a bicycle. On a windy day, the force from the wind can make riding hard work!

Racing cyclists want to go as fast as they can. They get a smoother and smaller shape by crouching down.

Racing cyclists can move at about 50 kilometres per hour.

?

1 How can you make your air resistance lower when you ride a bicycle?
2 Look at the photograph of the racing cyclist.
   a What is he wearing to help him to go faster?
   b How does this help?

A person's body is still not very smooth, even if they crouch down. Cyclists going for speed records use very special bikes.

Riders have to be helped into their bikes!

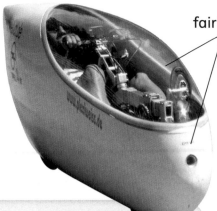

Bicycles like this can go up to 110 kilometres per hour. The smooth fairing helps air to flow around the bicycle.

fairing

The high speed bicycle has a much smaller area than a normal bicycle and rider.

?

3 Why does a high speed bicycle have a very low air resistance? There are two reasons.

Most forms of transport need streamlining if they travel fast. You can see this best if you look at different aeroplanes.

The Tiger Moth was designed in 1931. It has a top speed of just over 160 kilometres per hour.

The first aeroplane flight happened in 1903. Since then, engineers have designed bigger and faster aeroplanes. Faster aeroplanes need more powerful engines and better streamlining.

This Spitfire's top speed was 725 kilometres per hour. It was built in 1945.

?

4 Look at the photographs of aeroplanes.
  a Which aeroplane can fly the fastest?
  b Why do you think this aeroplane is the fastest? (*Hint:* there are at least two reasons.)
5 Describe the differences between the Tiger Moth and the Spitfire. You can make a list or a table if you like.
6 Find out who built and flew the first aeroplane with an engine.

The Blackbird aeroplane can fly at over 3000 kilometres per hour!

How can we make electrical circuits work?

This is a model lighthouse. The **bulb** makes light when **electricity** flows through it.

The bulb makes light.

The **wires** join the bulb and the battery. The **circuit** will only work if there are no gaps in it.

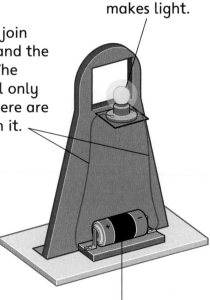

The **battery** provides the electricity.

?

1 a What does a battery do?
  b What does a bulb do?

This **circuit** will not work because there is a gap in it.

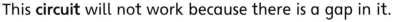

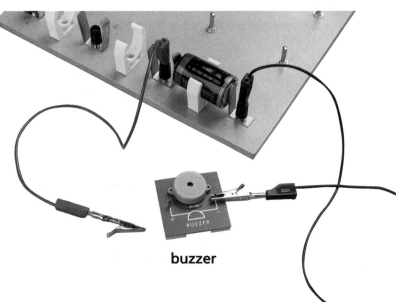

buzzer

Switches can be used to leave a gap in a circuit, or to close a gap in a circuit. The bulb is not working in this circuit because the switch is open. There is a gap in the circuit.

?

2 Look at the photograph of the circuit with a buzzer in it.
  a What does a buzzer do?
  b Why won't the buzzer work in the circuit in the photograph?
  c How could you make the buzzer work?

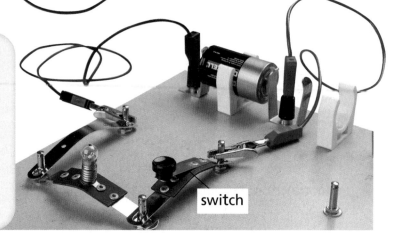

switch

This circuit is working because the switch is closed. There is no gap.

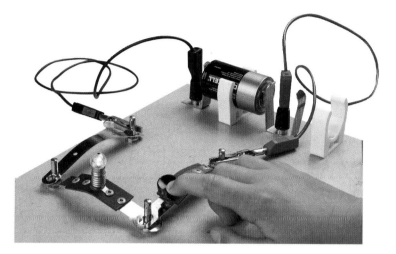

How can you make a switch?
- What will you need?
- How will you find out if it works?

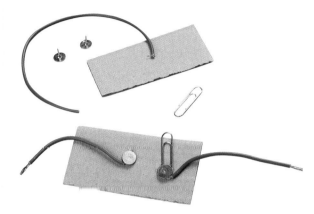

You win this game if you move the wire loop all the way along the bent wire without touching it. If you *do* touch it, the bulb lights up.
- How can you build a game like this?
- What will your circuit look like?
- What will you need in your circuit?

?

3 a What is a switch?
  b How does a switch work?
4 a Draw a picture of a circuit with a bulb and a battery in it.
  b Explain why the bulb in your circuit will light up.

Now you should know...
- What different parts of a circuit do.
- A circuit only works if there are no gaps.
- Switches can be used to turn circuits on or off.

What is mains electricity?

There are many things around us that need electricity to make them work. Some things need more electricity than others.

This MP3 player does not make a very loud sound. It only needs two small batteries.

This stereo is louder. It needs 8 batteries to make it work.

These loudspeakers make a lot of noise. They need a lot of electricity, so they have to be plugged into the **mains**.

All these things need **mains electricity**.

?
1 Why do loudspeakers need more electricity than an MP3 player?
2 Write down three things that need mains electricity to make them work.

Batteries do not provide much electricity. That is why they are safe to use in school for investigations. Mains electricity can be dangerous if you do not use it properly. It can give you an electrical shock, and may even kill you.

3 Why are batteries safer than mains electricity?
4 What can mains electricity do if you are not careful?

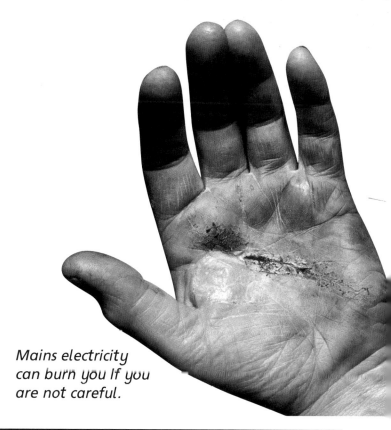

Mains electricity can burn you If you are not careful.

Using electricity safely

- Never touch the bare metal parts of plugs, or poke things into sockets.
- Never open up electrical equipment. You can sometimes get an electrical shock even if it is not still plugged in.
- Don't use anything electrical near water.
- Never play near places with warning signs like this.
- Do not use fishing rods near electricity wires.
- Do not play on railway lines or near them.

Danger of death

HS0753   www.egu.com

5 Why do electrical machines need switches?
6 Why must you be very careful with electrical equipment in the kitchen?
7 Why do you think you should not fly kites near electricity wires?

Now you should know...

- Some things need mains electricity to make them work.
- Mains electricity can be dangerous if it is not used properly.
- How to use mains electricity safely.

Why are there different kinds of switch?

Light switches help us to save electricity, because we can switch the light off when we do not need it.

This light switch is inside a fridge.

This video recorder has a lot of different circuits inside it. Some circuits make the video tape play, some make it fast forward or record, and so on. Each circuit has its own switch. These switches control what the video recorder does.

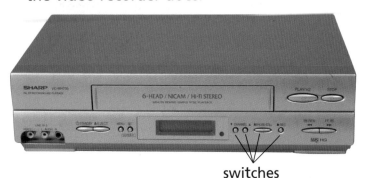

switches

Most light switches are fastened to a wall, but in the bathroom the switch is usually in the ceiling for safety. You work the switch by pulling on a long cord.

?

1 a Why do we need light switches inside fridges?
   b How do you think the switch works?
2 Why do you think bathroom light switches are in the ceiling?
3 a Why does a video recorder have lots of switches?
   b Write down the names of some other things that have lots of switches on them.

What does voltage tell us?

The torch on the right uses two small batteries. Each battery has 1.5 V written on its side. This means each battery provides 1.5 volts of electricity. The voltage is a way of measuring the power of the electricity. The torch needs 3 V of electricity altogether.

The torch below makes brighter light. It needs 6 V of electricity.

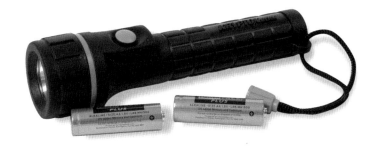

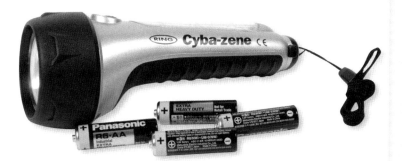

If the voltage is high enough, the electricity does not need wires. It will jump across a gap in a circuit!

Electricity from the mains is at 230 V. The higher the voltage, the more dangerous the electricity can be.

The electricity flowing in these power lines is at 400 000 volts!

1 What does 'V' stand for on a battery?

2 a Why does the small torch only need two batteries?

   b Why does the big torch need more batteries than the small torch?

3 a How much voltage does an electric kettle need?

   b Explain how you worked out your answer.

4 Why are power lines more dangerous than the electricity wires in your home?

How well does electricity pass through different materials?

This is a wire used in a circuit. It is made of metal covered in plastic.

P

How can you find out which materials can be used to make electrical circuits?

Electricity can flow through metals. We say that metals **conduct** electricity, and that metals are good **electrical conductors**. A circuit only works if all of it is made from materials that conduct electricity.

Electricity will not flow through materials like wood, plastic, rubber or glass. These materials are **electrical insulators**.

?

1 a Which materials will conduct electricity?
  b Which materials will not conduct electricity?
2 Zack has a gap in his circuit.
  a What could he use to join the gap to make his circuit work?
    A ruler
    B paper clip
    C string
  b Why do you think this?

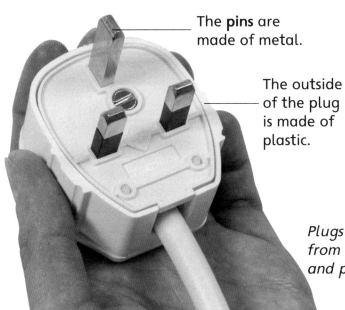

The **pins** are made of metal.

The outside of the plug is made of plastic.

Plugs are made from metal and plastic.

?

3 a Why are the pins in a plug made from metal?
  b Why is the outside of a plug made from plastic?

Circuits in machines are a bit more complicated than the circuits you make in school. Different wires have to be connected in the right places. This is a **cable** from a washing machine.

?

4 Look at the photograph of the washing machine cable.
  a How many wires are there inside it?
  b What do you think the wires are made of?
  c What do you think the wires are covered with?
  d Why do you think the coverings on the wires are different colours?

5

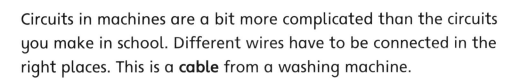

This switch is made of plastic, but there must be some metal inside it.

  a Do you think Anita is right?
  b Why do you think this?

Now you should know...

• Metals are electrical conductors. They are used for cables and wires.
• Plastics are electrical insulators. They are used for plugs and to cover wires.

What is inside a plug?

Most buildings have wires that carry electricity inside the walls. The wires are connected to sockets on the wall. We use plugs to connect electrical equipment to the sockets.

This is what a plug looks like inside.

The pins are made of metal. Each pin has a screw on top to hold the wire.

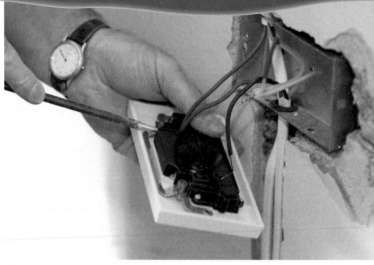

This man is putting a new socket onto a wall.

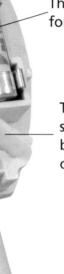

The fuse is for safety.

The cable grip stops the cable being pulled out of the plug.

The wires are covered in coloured plastic. The plastic has to be taken off the end of the wire before it is fastened to the pin.

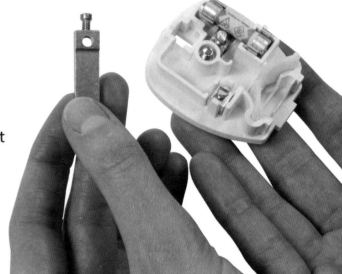

The metal pins stick through holes in the plastic case.

1 Describe a pin from a plug. Explain what the different parts of it do.
2 Why does the plastic have to be taken off the end of a wire before it is fastened to a pin?
3 The plug has a plastic cover that hides the wires inside it. Why is this important?

What happens if we use the wrong components?

A **component** is anything in a circuit, such as a bulb or a motor. Each component needs the right amount of electricity to make it work.

There is not enough electricity. The bulb is dim.

There is too much electricity. The bulb has broken.

The amount of electricity needed by the components must be matched to the amount of electricity produced by the batteries.

The bigger the number, the more electricity the bulb needs.

This number tells you how much electricity the battery produces.

?

1 What happens to a component if:
   a it does not get enough electricity
   b it gets too much electricity?
2 What will happen if you:
   a put the bulb and the battery in the photographs into a circuit
   b put a 6 V battery into a circuit with a 2.5 V bulb?

Now you should know...

- The amount of electricity a component needs is marked on it.
- Too much electricity can damage a component.
- If there is not enough electricity the component may not work.
- Components in a circuit need to be matched.

How can you change a circuit to make bulbs brighter?

P

How can you change the brightness of the bulbs in a circuit?
- Which parts of the circuit could you change?

What happens when you change the numbers of bulbs or batteries in a circuit?

Each battery in a circuit produces a certain amount of electricity. The more batteries you use, the more electricity you get.

The electricity in a circuit has to flow through all the components in the circuit. The more components there are, the harder it is for the electricity to flow.

There is more electricity flowing in this circuit.... than in this one.

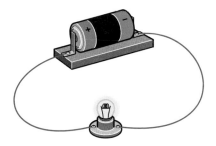 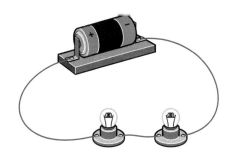

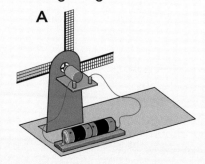 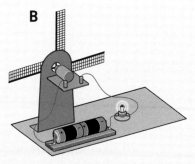

?

1 a How can you make bulbs brighter in a circuit?

b How can you make them dimmer (less bright)?

Now you should know...

- You can make bulbs brighter by using more batteries in a circuit.
- If you put more bulbs in a circuit they all get dimmer.
- If you put more motors in a circuit they all get slower.

The same thing happens if you use other components, such as motors. The more batteries you use, the faster the motor will turn.

?

2 a Which windmill will turn the fastest?

b Why do you think this?

A B

3 Write down two different ways of making:

a windmill B turn faster

b windmill A turn more slowly.

Glossary

°C
(*deg-grees sel-see-us*) The short way of writing 'degrees Celsius'.

air resistance A force that tries to slow down things that are moving through air.

backbone A set of bones that are in an animal's back. Another name for the spine.

bar chart A chart showing the numbers of things using bars.

battery Part of a circuit that provides the electricity.

biceps (*bye-seps*) A muscle at the front of your upper arm.

body temperature The normal temperature of a human (37 °C).

bone Hard, strong part found inside animals.

bulb (electricity) Something which lights up when electricity flows through it.

bulb (thermometer) The rounded end at the bottom of a thermometer.

buzzer Something that makes a noise when electricity flows through it.

cable (*cay-bul*) A thick wire that carries a lot of electricity. It usually has several different wires inside it.

circuit A battery, wire, and bulbs or other things, all joined in a complete loop.

component (*com-pO-nent*) Any part of a circuit.

conduct (*con-duct*) To allow electricity to flow.

consumer (*con-syou-mer*) An organism that eats other organisms.

contract (*con-tract*) When a muscle gets shorter and fatter it contracts.

degrees Celsius (*deg-grees sel-see-us*) The unit for measuring temperature. Often written as °C.

dim Not bright.

dissolve (*dizz-olv*) When a solid seems to disappear into a liquid we say that it dissolves.

electrical conductor (*el-eck-tri-cal con-duck-tor*) A material that lets electricity flow through it. Metals are electrical conductors.

electrical insulator (*el-eck-tri-cal ins-you-lay-ter*) A material that does not let electricity flow through it.

electricity Something produced by batteries that flows around circuits and makes bulbs and motors work.

evidence The information used to answer a question.

expand When something gets bigger it expands.

extinct Any kind of living thing that does not exist any more is said to be extinct.

fair test An investigation where you only change one thing, and you keep everything else the same.

filter	The thing used to catch a solid when you separate a solid from a liquid by filtering.
filtering	Using something with holes (a filter) to separate a solid from a liquid.
food chain	A diagram showing who eats who.
forcemeter	A piece of equipment containing a spring that is used to measure forces.
freezing	When a liquid turns into a solid.
freezing point	The temperature at which a liquid starts to freeze.
friction (*frick*-shun)	A force that tries to slow things down when two surfaces rub together.
grow	Get bigger.
habitat	The area where an organism lives.
ice	Frozen water. Ice is a solid.
invertebrate (in-**vert**-eb-rate)	An animal that does not have bones inside it.
joint	Part of your skeleton where bones meet and are moved by muscles.
key	A diagram that is used to find out the name of something.
ligament	A cord that connects two bones.
liquid (*lik*-wid)	Liquids flow and take up the shapes of the containers they are put in but do not change their volumes. Water is a liquid.
lubricant (**loob**-brick-ant)	A liquid that reduces friction.
lubrication (loob-brick-**ay**-shun)	When you add a lubricant to something to reduce friction.

mains	A short way of saying mains electricity.
mains electricity	Electricity supplied to houses and schools. It can be more dangerous than electricity from batteries.
measuring cylinder	A cylinder used to measure the volume of a liquid.
melting	When a solid turns into a liquid.
melting point	The temperature at which a solid starts to melt.
millilitre (*mill-lee-leet-ter*)	The units for volume. Shortened to ml.
mixture	Different materials jumbled together.
ml	Short way of writing millilitres.
muscle (*muss*-ull)	Part of your body that can move another part.
N	The short way of writing newtons.
newton	The unit of force (N).
oil	A thick liquid used to lubricate car engines and other machines.
organism (*or*-gan-izz-m)	A living thing.
pin	Part of a plug that conducts electricity.
pond dipping	Using a net or jar to collect small animals from a pond.
predator	An animal that hunts other animals to eat.
prediction (*pred-ik*-shun)	What you think the results of an investigation will be.

prey	An animal that is hunted by other animals.
property	A description of what a material is like. For example, brick is hard.
relax (ree-**lax**)	When a muscle gets longer and thinner it relaxes.
reproduce (**ree**-prod-yous)	Make new organisms.
reversible change (rev-**ver**-sib-el)	A change that can be turned back the other way. For example, ice can be melted and the water can be frozen again.
ribs	A set of bones inside an animal's chest.
room temperature	The usual temperature of a room (20 °C).
separating	Sorting a mixture into its different materials.
sieve (**siv**)	Something with holes in that you can use to separate things from a mixture.
sieving (**siv**-ving)	Using a sieve to separate things.
skeleton (**skell**-et-tun)	All the bones in an animal.
skull	The large bone inside an animal's head.
solid	Solids do not flow, do not change shape on their own, and do not change their volumes. Ice is a solid.
solidifying (sol-**lid**-ee-fy-ing)	Another word for freezing.
solution (soll-**oo**-shun)	The mixture formed when a solid dissolves in a liquid.
spine	A set of bones in an animal's back. Another name for the backbone.

streamlined	Having a smooth shape that air flows over easily.
switch	Something which can make a gap in a circuit, to turn other things on or off.
temperature (**temp**-rat-tyour)	How hot or cold something is. Usually measured in degrees Celsius (°C).
temperature sensor	Something that is attached to a computer to measure temperatures.
tendon	A cord that connects a muscle to a bone.
thermal conductor (**ther**-mal con-**duk**-tor)	Something that allows heat to go through it easily. Metals are thermal conductors.
thermal insulator (**ther**-mal **in**-syou-late-or)	Something that does not allow heat to go through it easily. Wood and plastic are thermal insulators.
thermometer (ther-**mom**-mit-er)	Something used to measure temperature.
triceps (**try**-seps)	A muscle at the back of your upper arm.
undissolved	If something has not dissolved we say that it is undissolved.
vertebrate (**vert**-eb-rate)	An animal that has bones inside it.
volume (**voll**-yoom)	The amount of space something takes up. Often measured in millilitres (ml).
water resistance	A force that tries to slow down things that are moving through water.
wires	Used to join parts of a circuit. Electricity flows through wires.